A little bit of Kismat, A little bit of Jalebi.

Muskaan Ayesha

Published by Eudaimonia Publishing Press, 2022.

Copyright.

Copyright © 2022 by Muskaan Ayesha.

All rights reserved. No part of this publication may be reproduced, distributed, or transmitted in any form or by any means, including photocopying, recording, or other electronic or mechanical methods, without the prior written permission of the publisher, except in the case of brief quotations embodied in critical reviews and certain other noncommercial uses permitted by copyright law. For permission requests, write to the publisher, addressed "Attention: Permissions Coordinator," at the email address below:

Muskaanayesha15@gmail.com

Table of Contents

This book is inspired by the Bollywood movie "Jalebi". Being a significant part of my youth, the movie focused on a carefree author named "Aisha". A similarity that is striking exists between this fictional character and I; and my friends often compared me to her. While I do relate to the character's personality, I also understand how many lovers may be able to relate to the story of the movie, and aside from that, stories that are similar. This book is a compilation of poems, essays and write-ups in English and Urdu that highlight the millions of love stories that have had no happy ending.

I would also like to confirm that a few of the Urdu poems in this book is from my previous book called "Musht-e-Khaak". The book mentioned is available upon request and it consists of the Urdu and English script of the poems alongside pictures to accompany them.

Dedication.

To all of our tooti phooti kismets.

Raazdaar.

Kitaab mein dil ke raaz likh kar
Hum chalay hai phir se
Dunya ko raazdaar bananay.

All that remained.

My sweetheart, you have left me confounded, struck by something I am not familiar with. You are the metaphor of heaven. Your existence that lured my soul to its feet, it no longer stands before me. I am beneath you, but you're not above me. And there is a ghazal that goes "Khabar-e-tahayyur-e-ishq sun" (listen to the confounding tale of love) ; my love, we are the tale, the entire chapter burning inside of my lungs. You found me in the abyss of my own bones, snuggled inside of my own breast, hidden inside of my own eyes. You took me home. You felt my heart swallow your essence like the sun itself settled into my chest. So aware of my fingertips, you could have carved your name into the fate of my palms. And then Siraj-ud-Din Aurangabadi wrote: "Na to tu raha, na to main raha, jo rahi so bekhabri rahi." (You did not remain, neither did I, all that remained was unawareness.).

Bad-naseebi.

Tumhain kya bataun bad-naseebi ke baray mein?
Jis ko Allah Allah kar ke paaya tha
Us ko Allah ne naseeb mein he nahi likha.

The truth about Jab We Met.

Everyone tells you that sometimes you've to go through hell to actually make it out of it. You have to lose something in life to find something even better. Like Geet found her Aditya after she missed her train. Let things to. Your Aditya finds his way to you after Anshuman leaves. But no one tells you that Geet missed her train more than once before she even introduces herself to Aditya. Life mein kabhi kabhi kuch paanay se pehle bohat kuch khona parta hai. No one tells you that Aditya goes months without asking Geet if she's happy, if she's living her dream life in the mountains. No one tells you that Geet lost herself in the entire process. No one tells you that Geet spends a portion of her life mourning the death of a love that didn't even exist. No one tells you that kuch instances mein jab tak Aditya ajata hai, tab tak to Geet he Geet nahi rehti. No one tells you that after the interval everything falls into place, only to fall back apart once the ending credits roll. There is no over-hyped song at the end of the movie; there are challenges even Aditya fails at. There is the 90% possibility that even he leaves. What people should be telling you is that the chances of never actually reaching your ultimate destination together is a lot more than the happy ending you expect. The only way to thoroughly make the best of life is to enjoy the journey. Make the most of every semi-colon in the book of love. At the end of the day, everything comes down to a full stop in any case; be it with Aditya or Anshuman.

Be-Wafai.

Tum se muhabbat hai to tumhara bharosa kartay hain.
Warna,
Be-wafai ko kismet ka naam nahi diya kartay.

Yeh Jawaani.

You are the exact moment between the interval of "Yeh Jawaani Hai Deewani" and the end of the New Year's countdown when Bunny realizes he's in love with Naina. You are the entire chorus of SubhanAllah, the symphony that has thousands in a chokehold. You are the feel-good mantra that reverberates within each echo of Kabira. You are the second of eureka when Naina finds a new person in herself, succumbing to the absence of her chashma. You are the very minute when Avi and Bunny hug each other after squarelling. Which is to ultimately say that: "Kuch logo ke sath sirf waqt beetane se hi sab kuch sahi ho jata hai" aur mere liye tum wahi ho.

Ankhain tumhari.

Tum ne dil ko daikha hai, dil mein nahi
Warna,
Ankhain tumhari kaafi qareeb se guzri hain.

Chaashni.

What is it about human nature that has such a strong hold on how we see unrequited love? A curse, a test, a tug-of-war you need to win with whatever power you hold in your little lungs, and, ultimately - a defeat that has wings, a paper plane that has no air, a museum with only silence in its feet, a fleeting moment of peace, a cheering sort of regret.

If you had one chance to settle in the creases of your lover's smile, or the crows feet at the corner of their eyes, or the dimple in their cheek, or the beard that you never got to touch, would you take it? Would you drop everything and run towards the very direction that they're standing in?

Maybe you're better off without them. Perhaps, they're better off without you. And one cold evening, you'll see them walking around with a child tugging at their sleeve, you'll see them at a street corner, you'll find them at the bakery with a box of jalebi in their hands. You'll look up, their eyes a warm, muddy mix of browns, and you'll smile. They were the Chaashni to your Jalebi, the color to the sweet, the goodbye in your hello. They were yours and yours are these memories.

Is that enough?

In Nazron se.

Ishq ko naseeb ki nazar lag gayi
Warna Khuda ki qasam
In nazron se tumhari nazar utara kartay thay.

All that matters.

You don't like the scent of henna
Or my favourite punjabi folks songs
But occasionally you call me yaar
And jigar ka tukra
And sometimes, that's all that matters

Dil tumhara deedar karnay ke liye betab para hai,
Han bas nazrain ijazat nahi daiti.

Growing up is really just catching a whiff of your old clothes in the cupboard or the scent of mustard oil and thinking of your grandmother's henna stained hair and the orange paranda you so vividly recall. It's your YouTube suggestions constantly putting up songs like Latthay Di Chaadar and Pasoori on your front page. Growing up is spending countless hours preparing a warm, hearty meal because eating out doesn't appeal to you anymore. It's the sudden cravings to eat Chai Paratha for breakfast and think of the plethora of green mangoes drying in the sun to make batches and batches of pickles. It's stopping at the refrigerator of a grocery store and thinking about how these green grapes don't compare to breaking fresh ones off of the tree before it was ready and then almost going into factory reset because of the sourness. It's having to Google the translation to 80% of Punjabi folk songs but memorizing the lyrics like you've just gotten your PhD in the language. It's realizing a Pandora bracelet could never make you feel at home like a bundle of glass churiya wrapped in newspaper. Growing up is finally understanding what your father meant whenever he said: "To move forward, you have to move backwards first." Because God knows, growing up means embracing the parts of your culture, heritage and blood that you previously felt ashamed of.

Tamasha.

Us ne ankhon mein ankhain dal kar kaha
"In ankhon ko faqat tum se muhabbat hai"
Haye,
Phir apni ankhon se kissi aur se ankhain yu milayi ke apna
tamasha ban gaya.

You were an absolute disaster in the most beautiful way possible, holding my heart like a marigold in your palms. Your eyes, the first part I saw of you, the ones that held my existence captive, your eyes that melted inside of the sun. You do not look at me with those eyes anymore. And our shared album has been collecting dust, like our memories will. I never met you, nor will I ever, perhaps. But when he calls me up, all I can think of is the way in which you'd say "jee, meri jaan" and by God, I am a mourning soul, aching for a person I fell in love with. A person I loved through little notes and late night whispers.

Tumhari Marzi.

Tumhari nazron mein gair janib dari ka silsila chal raha hai
Aur meri nazron mein abhi bhi sirf naam hai tumhara.
Ab isse tum mera ishq samjho ya sabar,
Tumhari marzi.

Out of Reach.

The strangest thing about falling in love with someone is remembering even the most insignificant parts of them. Like the way you held my hand for the first time in your car, and the inevitable feeling of knowing that you would be the reason I believed in love again. Like the time you put your ring onto my finger, and the moment you rested your head on my chest, and the heartbeat beneath my ribcage almost halting. Or the Jacaranda trees we passed, your words encasing me in something heavenly. Like the way in which you looked at me in the mirror, or called me beautiful exactly 4 times in an hour. Like the way you closed your eyes when my fingers wrapped around themselves in your hair. Or how you kissed my forehead. Like the way in which you type certain words in your texts, and the sound of your laughter. Like the nights you visited my dreams, and all the "I miss you's" you said to me inside of the well of my own consciousness. It's remembering the night you told me not to leave you, and I told you not to give me a reason to - when what I should have said was... don't leave me too. It's remembering how I waited to see you so I could tell you that I love you, and how you held that opportunity out of reach.

Kaabil.

Tujhe tab ishq kiya tha jab tu ishq karne ke kaabil nahi tha,
Ab kaabil ban gaya hai to mujhe apne kaabil na samjha.

Kothde uthe kothda.

You're on my mind when Ali Sethi says "Chan kithan...... raat ve?" and these thoughts beg to know who you're sharing your whispers and your silence with now. Granted, I have closed the door that you had once walked through; just as you walked out of it. And yet, my dear Moon, Kothde utthe kothda, terrace upon terrace, and under this rainy evening, I think about you.

Us ne janay ke baad kaha,
Ab aur na rona.
Usko kehna,
Kissi ke marnay par teen din sog manaya jaata hai,
Ye to phir apna janaza hain.

But when you say "Meri Jaan" you sound like my favourite folk songs and a cup of chai from the street corner. To be with you in the streets of Lahore, breaking mulberries from small trees on our way to the Sunday market. I'd take you to the food stall across the train track in the city I lived in and race you to the abandoned park with a bridge too fragile to run across. We'd visit a fortress and share a single kulfi on our way back. So do not leave. There'd be a Mohammed Rafi song playing in a random Rickshaw and I'd look over to you when he says: "Abhi na jao chod kar, ke dil abhi bhara nahi." But it wouldn't be the entire truth: For do not go now and do not go ever; this heart of mine will never be full of you.

Kamzori.

Khuda se baat karnay ka waqt maanga tha hum ne
Sajday se sar utha kar daikha
To tum chalay gaye thay
Isko khuda ki marzi samjhu?
Ya tumhare pyaar ki kamzori?

Twin Flames.

We're both born of the same star, so close in proximity within the spectrum of time. You wish me first, and I wish you after. But you were before me, and I existed only months ahead. You're the altar, the bell, the entire wedding vow compressed into a soul; a soul I have thought of inhaling. Almost like twins, but we could never be twin flames. And that is the greatest flaw in our stars. That is the greatest flaw in our palms.

Jism ka Sauda.

Jin bazaron mein jism biktay hain
Un bazaron mein dil ka sauda kaise karu?

At 21, I water myself down, I hold on to anyone that looks at me. At 21, I shrink myself to fit into a man's pocket. At 21, I don't care about being the only one - only about being the favorite one. At 21, I feel a scream lodged inside of my throat. It aches to be silent. At 21, there are no dreams or aspirations; there is only the need to be loved.

Aks.

Ankhon se to noch du tera aks,
Magar sun,
Dil ka kya karu?
Yahan bhi sirf tera naam hain.

Dear Shams of Tabriz.

Dear Shams of Tabriz,

I know that you are well aware of the mark you have left behind but the world does not know. The world and all that is in it does not know of the 40 days of seclusion that you spent with Rumi and that the myriad of poetry they read by the poet of love was written in your honor. 3000 to be precise, maybe more, perhaps a little less. But there is a lifetime of emotions embedded into these poems that the world barely even relates to you. Dear Shams, you had taught Rumi the meaning of love and life and the secrets of the universe. I am forever indebted to you for the person that I have become through your words. As a poet, I am in awe of the stanza after stanza that Rumi scribbled in his life but it is you that has taught me the art of being a human, an empath, a vessel of light and brilliance. I do not understand why you rejected the love of Kimia, but there must have been some wisdom to it just as there was wisdom in your compassion towards the drunk and the sober, the modest and the prostitute, the able and disabled, men of health and the man suffering from leprosy. Shams, you are the sun in the world that is used to being born to darkness and death. Rumi is the pen but you are the feeling behind it. All that we learn of love from Rumi, was love that spoke your name. Did you leave Konya and take your last breath in Khoy? Or did a man of hate force your life out of your lips? I do not know, but I will not look to blame because you had once said: "A good man complains of no one; he does not look to faults," and for that, my warm heart will forever remain content.

Samjhota.

Tum kya samjhota karnay chale thay mujhe bina ishq apna bana kar?
Tum se muhabbat mangi thi
Saath to kissi na kissi se mil he jaata hain.

Love is beyond the realms of this world. Beyond the body and soul. Love is praying at 3am and in prostration while your ego is buried in the soft creases of a prayer mat, it's praying while the call to prayer goes and while fasting, it's praying when your eyes awaken in the middle of the night and before sunset on a Friday. Love is entrusting your beloved to God and having faith that he will return to you.

Love is the sweet pomegranate with a seed from heaven and the waves of the ocean overlapping into your lungs. Love without purpose is a disaster in the making but love with the right intentions is a symphony so sweet it follows you wherever you go. Love is looking at the world and trusting that God has the best of plans.

Love is the tombstone of intellect but the birthstone of ecstasy.

Muhabbat azmana

Tum se roothna bhi chor diya
Tumhe khonay ke khauf se
Is tarha azmaya hain main ne apni muhabbat ko.

The flute in his palm whistled without his lips, like the music was made for his hands. The anklets of women running down the palace echoed into the horizon. The sun was setting into colors of honey and peaches and the waves of a pink river. A peacock fluttered its feathers open, flaunting the kaleidoscope colors into the tiny mirrors embedded into her dress. The rainbow hues blinded him as he saw her walk down the stairs. Her scarf lay settled on her head, a single strand of hair singing against her cheek. The embroidery on the material felt like a crown made specifically for her. He put his flute down, jumping off of the low balcony that he sat on. His smile reached towards her soul. Somewhere in the distance, a merchant drove off on his bicycle, the bell ringing in a soothing melody. The spring flowers released their scent into the air as the two lovers met eye to eye. He takes her hand in his, subtly stroking her palm with his thumb. "Is my fate written in this lines?" He asks, as he continues staring at her palm. "If it isn't, I'll make a line of your name on it myself," she whispers as the last twitching sight of the sun goes down.

Usse Haq Hai.

Haq hai usse ke mera naam pukaar ke
Mujhe wapas bej de
Bas yahi khawahish hai k wo mjse haq na cheene usse pukaarne
ka

I have seen myself as a tyrant and believed that God did not listen to me, that the sun would rise for everyone else but my eyes and the moon felt heavy in my palms. The stars breathed suffocation into my lungs and I knew, I just knew that I needed to find a way out. Despair is a common village for me to stop at, and every resident of it knows my name. But I have sworn to save myself and I have felt the orchids bloom inside of me just as I started to accept my life as the masterpiece of God. My face appeared to me as a creation so carefully molded by the perfect creator and the flaws in it stared back at me like lavender in a never ending field. The thing about love is that it is eternal when it is for your creator. Love blooms from all four corners of your soul when you hand your faith over to God. God is affection and love, God is love and forgiveness, God is mercy and happiness and so am I.

Rangreza.

Aansu mein agar rang hotay
Allah ki qasam
Tum mere rangreza hotay.

"But what is love?" She asked him. He smiled, in sadness, in regret, in contemplation perhaps. Looking out of the small circular window, he saw the children running freely in the fields across. "Love is sacrifice. You know how the minute a soldier goes to war, the chances of death are physically engraved onto his uniform? A soldier is ready to sacrifice his life for his country. Love is knowing that you might have to sacrifice your heart at the battlefield and it's falling anyway. Love is waking up everyday and putting your uniform on, knowing that you might die that day. Love is subtle sighs escaping as you bid them farewell and the sound of your beloved dancing across your ears. Love is holding a handgun in one hand and a holy script in the other. Love is death. Slow, sweet, soft death." She looked at him in concern. "Would you die for love?" she whispered. "To become a martyr for my darling? Why ever would I turn down that opportunity?"

My Lord.

And the sun in your eyes, my beloved, your heartbeat is echoing in my chest like these twin hand drums crooning behind the pathway of your dimple. The harmonizing sound of your tongue, leaving goosebumps on my skin. The way your fingertips breathe life into my soul.

Lord, my Lord, how have you created a man that is the image of love and symphonies? And you let him stride towards me like a fallen angel. My Lord, you have left me speechless with this creation of yours. No poem can justify this aching pull towards him. I desire to hold his eyes in my heart, like he holds my heart in his palms.

These shadows dance across his eyebrows, the wrinkles of difficulty tracing his forehead, erase them. Erase all of the ache in his soul, and place them into my lungs. I will breathe the pain like I breathe your name, my Lord. And I will pray for his wellbeing like I pray for his name.

Majboor.

Majboori hain to majboor rahainge
Faqat
Apni muhabbat pe keechar uchaalne nahi denge.

A love like that.

There are very rare instances when love leaves the ephemeral realm and settles into the eternal realm. Rare, because love like this isn't just passionate, it's consuming. It's so consuming that it holds every part of you captive. And when a love like that occurs, it ends in either one of these two ways: in insanity, madness, complete chaos or two, in the love of God.

This kite of ours.

Whatever pain this heart holds, I'll clutch between these ribs. This kite of ours, this is an ode to this kite of ours. The thread is broken, my love. This kite of ours. The thread is broken.

This repetition, repetitive repetition, like the oaths you broke repetitively. Our destination was in front of us, but your feet shook and trembled. The way your hands moved away from mine. This is an ode to this kite of ours. The thread is broken, my love.

This sky of mine, this sky bare of the moon. You left this sky. You left the winds that whispered your name. This is an ode to this kite of ours. The thread is broken, my love. This kite of ours. The thread is broken. Broken. Broken. Broken. This repetition. This repetitive repetition like my breath repetitively stopping.

Ode to my grandmother.

Ode to my grandmother
And the sight of her always wearing orange
To the way she'd climb the stairs even when she couldn't.
Ode to my grandmother
And her hands tinged in yellow
All the turmeric she embellished on green mangoes
How the sun watched the fruit dry from above
Ode to my grandmother
The way she tied her money in a knot at the edge of her scarf
And her hands reaching for bread from the night before without
complaint
Ode to my grandmother
And how she sipped her tea from a ceramic bowl
Turning it in round circles as it swished and splashed until it
cooled down
Ode to my grandmother
And her braided hair thick with mustard oil
Her height that almost justifies mine
And her love that overlapped the ocean itself.
Ode to my grandmother
And how I didn't see her take her last breath
Two years after her death and it finally sinks in
That I'll never get to do an ode for my grandmother
To my grandmother.

Dear Sassi (a reference to Rangreza).

Dear Sassi, at first I thought you reminded me of myself, of my indecisiveness, of the rebellion whispering in my blood, of the consequences reaped from the actions I took in rage. But you define the love my lover feels for me, or the lack of it. You find someone better, someone who you can't have, and you lean a possessive shoulder over them. They do not love you, you learn later. And when you learnt it, I cried with you. Sobbed, for a week. I do not wish to see myself in that ear-shattering, throat-croaking, chest aching situation.

He is my Sassi and I am his Qasim. I blow color into his existence, the wall for him to fall back on. I am hushed and silent in my love, ever-willing to destroy my ego for his own. Qasim, the puppet. Sassi, my lover is my puppeteer. I am falling at his command, and yet he acts as if he doesn't command me. This dalliance is existent and yet it doesn't seem to exist. I am far-reaching for the sound of his laughter. The beautiful, vile, selfless and yet selfish cacophony of his life. His palms that hold my strings.

He is not wrong, no. Like you weren't, Sassi. But the Sassi in my lover is just as fickle, he harbours thoughts and dreams beyond me, above me and beneath me and I am in none of those. Yet, as those dreams crash, the Qasim in me struggles to find every shattered piece and caress life into it again.

I am my own enemy and he is his own traitor and in the end, the Qasim in me might settle for someone better but the Sassi in him will always love me, me, me. And I, I will respect my responsibilities and echo his name in this four wall ribcage that holds only his heart. Pain, it is pain that I do not wish for either of us.

And so, dear, Sassi, what will it take for him to realise I am his Qasim before it is too late?

Mehram.

You left, in haste. An ever-present cloud of ache hovering above me. I do not reach out to you, in fear of rejection. There are no walls between us, except for our own minds. And this mind of mine, believing you to be my beloved, is as shattered as the floor keeping us above water. I listened to "Mehram" on repeat, shrieking in cacophinic silence. The foundation of my heart falling beneath my feet. I have lost my Saeeban... if you ever were mine to begin with.

I left, in haste. An ever-present cloud of relief hovering above me. You will not reach out to me, slave to your pride. There are no walls between us, except for our own indifference. And this indifference of mine, believing you to be a mistake, is as heavy as the water suffocating me. I listened to "Mehram" on repeat, shrieking in cacophinic silence. The remains of my heart scraping against my heels. I have lost myself.... if I was ever mine to begin with.

Shiddat.

Tumhe kho kar bhi paa liya
Is shiddat se chaha hain tumhe
Tum to chalay gaye,
Magar
Dil tera idhar he reh gaya
Is shiddat se chaha hain tumhe.

Bismillah, I am writing the end of a chapter that never began. This is what we have come to, what our love has come to. I believe you had come into my life for a reason beyond my understanding, and it may take a century to fathom the intense familiarity I found in your voice. But this is the choice of Allah. You have not hurt me and I have not hurt myself either. I am content with the decision that our destiny has made. Kismet, like we joked about. This is our kismet, my love. I am a fickle human, I will find an abode elsewhere, as will you. This is how it ends. Fi aman Allah. I entrust you to Allah, my little gold star.

Mistaani.

You called me your "Mistaani", your "Jaan". Held onto me like a lifeboat, whispering my name back to me every night. When you marry the love of your life, may you lose memory of me. For in my heart, despite it all, I know that we were soul mates, made of the same substance with the same soil. And I am content with that. I could never regret the best two months and some days of my entire existence, nor could I regret the countless hours you spent healing my whole being. But love is a silly little tragedy, and when I think about it, all I actually really regret is never asking you what "Mistaani" meant.

Something you've never had.

You can't feel the loss of something you never had; you can't feel the lack of something that you never experienced. And that was life before him. But then he gave me unconditional love. And he showed me what it feels like to be overwhelmingly happy. And now nothing compares to that. And I will forever feel the loss of the potential we once had.

Love is all but love.

If you look into the depth of every poem I have written, every part of me that I have laid naked within these words, you should find a cry for help. There is a scream inside of these sentences, a failed form of escapism. It all comes back to this - to the revolting truth of our existences - love is all but love; love is lust gathered and wrapped in sunshine. When night comes, all pretense falls, fails, uncovers the truth that is: love is all but love. And I am standing at the center of this poem, stripping off this love inside of me. Where there is this chest of mine - and that is all it is - this chest of mine with a heartbeat so shallow and a house on fire. Nothing uncovers that. And I am stone hearted, unable to fathom the silhouette of the woman in the mirror. Senseless, like this cacophony of words, senseless enough to know that ... love is all but love.

Memories.

How does knowing a person for two months equate to forgetting them for five months? And I can't reach out to you, not a single aching atom in my body would permit that. I have burnt every picture of you. But I do think of the woman lucky enough to call you hers. I don't believe that it should have been me, and months have gone by since I've cried over you. I let these moments swallow me, days go by and all I listen to is the playlist with all your favourite songs. And you are the jukebox to this dance called life. I don't think about your silly messages, and you're no longer the "worst best friend reporting in". You're the worstestest, and I mean that in the bestestest way possible. If there has been one person that has made me the happiest, it has been you, my little gold star. May you never read that, may you never know how much you meant to this ocean of disaster that I am. I promise you, I absolutely hate every part of you, in a way that makes me sing out to every single song from every single rom-com that has a feel good vibe. You're not here to scream at the top of your lungs with me, but I have heard you whisper to them, and that has been enough.

Two months too short.

You were a tale two months too short in this lifetime of moments but your hands will forever be the only thing to ground this renegade of a soul enclosed inside of me. So when you spend your nights with another, I hope you never come across the playlist you made of all my favourite songs, and the memory of my laughter never keeps you up. It is enough that I will always think about the hum in your voice on the other end of the call, but I am alone in my thoughts and the weight of another does not forbid me from the silence in this love. And I hope you never saved the letters I had written for you with the nostalgic thought that sounds a little like "just in case." It goes without saying that I have saved yours. And maybe a few months from now I'll toss away their ashes but you will always be the first person to have written those to me and I will always be the last person to be the fleeting object of your affection.

And all I really wanted from you
Was to whisper to me
"Gussa choro ab, meri jaan".

To have a Jaggi/To be a Jaggi.

To be admired and adored. To be prayed for, ached for. But it is I, I am the one that has loved you with this Shiddat. In passion, in despair, in desire and to death. To swim across the ocean, fall into your lap, you are the oxygen I am lifeless without. There is a distance between us. Our destinations are just as different as our paths. And by God, if you called me your Muskaan, your muskurahat, I would have fallen to my knees, placed my heart into your hands. But this bitter moment is witness, all you have been is a sin, the punishment to it, and the court of law. And all I have been is a wilting shadow, drowning in this shiddat.

The flames of love.

You have come to me like a dream on a unknown path. I have been uneasy, without reason, without understanding, are you here to show me how to love or how to leave? You are the epitome of distaste. The moment between love and hate. And when Ali Sethi says "Ek main tha aur thi tanhaayi" in "Ishq", I thought about the tedious seconds in your presence. The uncertainty, the baffling ache. You have given wind to the flames of love in this heart of mine, and kept yours as cold as your fingertips. And I have found my loneliness in your eyes. But your loneliness, and my loneliness and the interlocking of our hands will never lead to ... anything but a lifetime of loneliness. That is what I have found, and what I have felt in our last fleeting goodbyes.

Rukhsati.

And when you would have signed your nikaah papers, this heart of mine will clench in silence, falling into a million pieces, gracing your feet. But I will pray for happiness, and hers, and mine in an abyss, hiding beneath rubble somewhere. There will be no rukhsati, except for my love leaving this chest of mine, calling me a traitor for I could not fulfill the desires that brewed within. And when she calls your name, it will not sound like me. She will not get the nights of whispers, and the mornings of laughter, and the sighs of young love. But she will have something I could never. She will have your last name. So perhaps, I have lost. And she has won. And your victory has been in my loss.

Malal.

Is baat ka gham nahi hain ke tumhe chor kar jana para
Malal ye hain ke tumhe chorne mein dair kardi maine.

Tumhe thaam kar rakhna bhi jaise koi gunah tha
Malal ye hain ke hum khushi khushi gunahgar bante gaye.

Tumne to kabhi mujhe apna samjha he nahi
Malal ye hain ke hum tumhe apna sab kuch samajhte gaye.

Jalebi.

To be called jalebi as I make my way into your arms. To have your palms plastered upon my palms as you look into my eyes. There is a street corner and piping hot sweetness on a stall somewhere, but the sugar in your eyes hold more strength. The burnt honey dribbling down my gaze, almost as if teasing me. I told you I saw galaxies in you, and you, you saw a mere atom in me. But that is all there is in this silence today. You had never loved me. And I had loved you enough for the both of us - until I could not love for either of us anymore.

The story of Aysh.

Ayesha: She who lives//The one who lives. But I am soulless, a body of nothingness. There is silence in these bones and dust in these lungs. And when they call me Aysh, the one that is eccentric, the one that is full of life, and chaos and rebelliousness. When they call me Aysh, the one that is a renegade, the one that firmly believes in grabbing the Sun by the throat, they do not see the Ayesha that is a vessel of grave sand, that holds her bleeding tongue in her fist and slams door shut because they did not open to the right worlds. They do not see me.

Tum kehte to tumhare liye jaan haazir kar dete,
Magar afsos
Tumne chaha bhi to sirf mujhe naam se,

You feel like garam chai, with a hint of elaichi wrapped within each sip. You are the last burfee on the tray, covered in a single dried rose petal. You are the sound of my payal against the concrete floor and the scent of the gajray in my hair. You are the simple pleasures in life. Looking into your eyes feels like the paan wali dukaan and the sound of "Main koi aisa geet gaun" playing in the near distance. You are the chaand shining in the sky after a storm, and the aandhi that brings sweet scented winds with it. Your laughter is the sound of my churiya against my wrists and the magic of a tabla. You feel like passing by a mazaar, inhaling the overwhelming aroma of roses. You feel like sleeping on a chaarpai under the stars and listening to Noor Jehan on a cold evening. Which is to ultimately say that you feel like heaven on earth.

Don't miss out!

Visit the website below and you can sign up to receive emails whenever Muskaan Ayesha publishes a new book. There's no charge and no obligation.

https://books2read.com/r/B-A-VHJK-SKSZB

BOOKS2READ

Connecting independent readers to independent writers.

Did you love *A little bit of Kismat, A little bit of Jalebi.*? Then you should read *Epitaph*[1] by Muskaan Ayesha!

In life, there are a myriad of emotions we want to let go off, a plethora of feelings we cannot let go of and a few people we are forced to let go of. This is a memoir to all of these. This is a dedication to everything that has left us behind and everything about ourselves that we lost on the way.

1. https://books2read.com/u/49kQRY

2. https://books2read.com/u/49kQRY

Also by Muskaan Ayesha

The Bird Handbook for Poets
Me, Her, the Ocean and the Stars
30/12/2020
Handful Of Dust
Epitaph
A little bit of Kismat, A little bit of Jalebi.

About the Author

Muskaan Ayesha is a literature connoisseur that has several poetry books under her belt. She began her writing journey at the age of 16 and has since then written news articles, non-academic articles, poetry, and a novel.